Punch Your Way To Fitness

Ian Oliver

snowbooks
LONDON

Copyright © 2007 Ian Oliver

Ian Oliver asserts the moral right to be identified as the author of this work.

All rights reserved.

Proudly published in the UK, in 2007, by:

Snowbooks Ltd.

120 Pentonville Road

London

N1 9JN

Tel: 0207 837 6482

Fax: 0207 837 6348

email: info@snowbooks.com

www.snowbooks.com

Small Publisher of the Year 2006

British Library Cataloguing in Publication Data

A catalogue record for this book is available from the British Library.

ISBN 13 978-1-905005-314

www.snowbooks.com

Printed and bound by J. H. Haynes & Co. Ltd., Sparkford

CONTENTS

DEDICATION

Dedicated to all instructors, staff and students (especially my Monday Mobs) of the Bob Breen Academy past and present.

To Brenda, Marge, Sue, Jimmy, Tom, Glen, Ellie, Joe, Charmaine, Clare, Danny and Ronnie, and all the Walkers and Mitchells.

To the memory of John McDavid, Laura Logan, Andrew 'Wink' Walker, Roy Beckworth, Johnny Bird, Johnny Hill, Mag and Archie, Dolly and Ernie, and F.S.O.

Ian Oliver is a veteran boxing trainer based in Hackney, North London. He is the author of the bestselling book *Boxing Fitness*.

ACKNOWLEDGEMENTS

Pete Drinkell (again) for his terrific photography.

Everybody at Snowbooks.

Bob and Judy Breen for allowing me the use and abuse of The Bob Breen Academy, Hoxton Square.

All my Monday students at The Academy.

Terry Barnett for his massive input on combinations.

Everybody who modelled for photos (all instructors and students of The Bob Breen Academy, and The Dartford Academy).

Ann and Sandra, my top salesgirls.

Wayne Rowlands, Owen Ogbourne, Dave Birkett and Steve Wright for all their help.

Preface

In *Boxing Fitness* I advocated the use of focus pads but could only, given the scope of the book, devote a few pages to the actual technique and benefits to be derived from their use. I consider focus pads to be an integral part of training both for boxing and mixed martial arts, for the following reasons:

1. **Technique:** Working on the light or heavy bag can improve speed and power but does not offer the challenge that focus pads can provide, with regard to the range and variation of punches – especially when dictated by an experienced coach.

2. **Motor skills:** i.e. the ability to utilise skeletal muscles efficiently. Working on focus pads encourages strong hand/eye co-ordination as well as improved upper and lower body synchronization.

3. **Fitness and dexterity:** Working on the pads can improve reflexes, endurance, strength, stamina and balance, especially with regard to specific footwork skills.

4. **Range of training skills:** Can be adapted for use in most martial arts that employ striking. Advanced students can utilise pads into training for blows from the elbows, feet and knees.

For these reasons I feel focus pads need and deserve to be covered in some depth in order for both trainers and trainees to derive the maximum benefit from their use. What I have set out to do in this book is to try to expand the use of focus pads as far as I know, mainly aimed at acquainting newcomers to their use, but also hopefully introducing some techniques and drills to experienced coaches.

The people who introduced me to focus pads were former Southern Area Featherweight Champion George Carroll and the late, and undeniably great, Dave Thomas, both coaches at the long defunct London Polytechnic Boxing Club. Dave was the former European Heavyweight Champion at amateur level; my respect for them both remains boundless.

Since those very early days I have gleaned as much information as I can on pad training with the help of such redoubtable martial artists as Bob Breen, Terry Barnett (who provided many of the combinations in the book), Dave Birkett and my colleagues Wayne Rowlands and Owen Ogbourne, all of whom I am proud and extremely fortunate enough to include as friends.

Apart from the technical and conditioning aspect of pad work there is, at base, something refreshingly uplifting, at times, about bashing the living daylights out of an inanimate object to dispel the frustration and stress of modern life, and, if this alone works for you, then I hope you will enjoy working on focus pads.

Introduction

1. Introduction

Hitting for fitness

Many of the people who train for boxing never use weights or organised resistance training, but are able to become remarkably fit by merely running, skipping and punching bags and pads – traditional boxing fitness methods – which bears testimony to the efficacy of this particular training. The main reason for the growing popularity in following this kind of regime usually stems from the simple fact that so many enjoy training in this manner, while they would not derive a similar pleasure from weights or aerobic forms of training. The gains are manifold.

I am fairly sure that most people, even if they have never entered a gym, know what punch bags are. They need little explanation. More people are finding out about focus pads as their usage becomes more widespread. There is a common belief among many of us engaged in the fitness industry that everything 'comes round again' but I never thought I would see the resurrection of medicine balls (especially of the big leather variety), let alone punch bags and focus pads.

Focus pads are, for the uninitiated, pads of dense foam encased in leather, canvas, or a synthetic material, backed with a glove to allow one person, ('the holder') to hold them whilst a training partner ('the hitter') punches them.

Focus pads are also referred to as 'Hook and Jab Pads', harking back to the days when they would only be found only in boxing gyms; nowadays they are used in many fitness establishments. It should always be borne in mind this is a dynamic, forceful and vigorous mode of training, and safety must be paramount. Poor technique can quite easily result in injuries to the hands, wrists or shoulders. Whether holding or hitting, sound technique is crucial.

Focus pads are most commonly used in boxing and the martial arts, but are an excellent, yet underrated, support exercise for a number of sports, given the benefits to upper and lower body co-ordination, arm and shoulder strength and endurance, as well as upper body conditioning. For anybody who simply wants to improve his or her fitness, and is game enough to take on some demanding anaerobic work, this form of training can be both enjoyable and refreshing.

Focus pads allow the hitter to attempt any punch (or combination of punches) as a close rehearsal of the 'real thing', sparring. Anybody considering sparring, even light sparring, should spend time training on focus pads to learn about technique, range and timing.

The holder has to be proficient, or both participants will be wasting their time. Padwork teaches the holder a great deal about power and movement. The holder should always imagine what his or her own defence would be against the punches 'fielded' on the pads.

Mobility is an important factor: very little boxing takes place 'toe to toe' for prolonged periods of time. All movement should be lively and imaginative, to emulate authentic ring moves.

Punchbags

If the gym you train at has a punch bag, or if you have a punch bag at home, it is most likely to be of the 'hanging' variety, usually about 3 or 4 feet long, or a free-standing 'bag', usually about 6 feet high, both bags being tubular in shape. As far as consistency goes, the bag should be very firm but not rock-like. I liken a good punch bag to a good hard-boiled egg, in as much as it must not be too soft or too hard: rather, 'just right'.

Boxing and martial arts gyms invariably have a greater variety of bags, many of which are designed to allow more varied punching. Watch out for the following.

I. FLOOR TO CEILING BALL

An inflated ball suspended from above and below by springy but strong elasticised cord. Every strike sends the ball off at an unpredictable angle, calling for improved reactionary and timing skills. It also tests defensive skills, as failure to move the head after hitting can lead to the ball hurtling back at a rate of knots which can surprise an unwary hitter. It simulates the movement of an extremely elusive moving target, very much akin to the way an opponent would move the head to avoid your punches. Be warned – I once witnessed the ball 'hitting back' and flooring an inexperienced user, so make sure you move your head off-line with every blow.

2. HOOK & UPPERCUT WALL PAD

There is very little 'feedback' from this static pad, which provides excellent opportunities to improve hooking and uppercutting skills, but straight punches can also be included in combinations.

3. ANGLE BAG

Angle bag is just one of the names attributed to this versatile hanging bag, a 'Peanut bag' being another, unsurprisingly, given its shape. Lends itself to every punch, whereas uppercutting is tricky on a straight tube-shaped bag.

4. MAIZEBALL

Unlike the inflated football-like floor-to-ceiling ball, this is a heavy duty suspended ball extremely dense in nature, good for building up punching power on a moving, albeit slow-moving, target.

5. MAIZEBAG

Much bigger version of the above but extremely dense and unresponsive, ideal for big punchers and potential big punchers, but more suited to experienced hitters, not much fun for beginners. Experienced or otherwise, the hands need to be wrapped for this piece of kit.

Teardrop and uppercut wall bag

6. SPEEDBALL

You'll hear it before you see it if somebody is using it, due to the staccato sound it makes as it repeatedly strikes its wooden framework above.

Seen in every boxing film but, due to the nature of the way it is struck, with light repetitive blows, more of a training tool than an aid to improving technique. Builds endurance, particularly in the shoulders and arms.

7. TEARDROP BAG

An aid to improving all the punches, as the bag swings to and fro and from side to side, calling for improvised punching. Great training for body blows. Good target for the shovel hook.

8. STANDBALLS

An old favourite of boxing gyms but now something of an endangered species as they have to be bolted to the floor (unless the base has the weight of an anvil). They are very good for teaching novices straight punches, particularly the jab.

9. HEAVY BAG & LIGHT BAG

Heavy Bag

This is where the hitter can improve dynamic power with powerful blows on this solid bag. Go for deliberate full-blooded punches as the bag swings towards you, to get maximum effect. The arm must be kept straight as you make contact with the knuckle part of the glove; if your wrist is cocked it is quite easy to injure the wrist. With this in mind it is advisable to wrap the hands for this bag. Great for both long and close range punches.

Light Bag

As the name would suggest this bag is going to swing about a lot more.

Calls for fast punching combinations while encouraging deft footwork to move around the bag, working on angles. Ideal for novices, the perfect introductory punch bag.

10. FREE-STANDING BAG

Tall, well-padded, solid piece of equipment which is totally static, but does allow the hitter to move 360 degrees around it. Popular in gyms as they can be wheeled away and brought out when required and need no fixings. The supporting floor needs to be substantial, however, as the large base needs to be filled with water or sand for stability, making it extremely heavy.

WHY TRAIN ON PADS AND BAGS?

» **Improves upper body strength and tone**

» **Increases stamina and speed**

» **Improves co-ordination and power**

» **Improves cardiovascular fitness**

» **Improves anaerobic fitness and endurance**

» **Relieves stress**

» **Improves bone density, lessening risk of osteoporosis**

» **Burns body fat**

» **Improves balance and mobility**

» **Boxing skills provide the most basic form of self-defence.**

To the bone

A key reason to train on focus pads is to improve bone density. Punching pads and using the footwork that must be used to train effectively build stronger bone and retard osteoporosis. When performing exercise involving rebounding and impacting – in other words, load-bearing activities – muscle pulls on bone, which stimulates increased blood supply, delivering nutrients including calcium which in turn increase bone density.

Dynamic evidence

The 'European Journal of Applied Physiology' (volume 60, number 5) includes an article in its Biomedical and Life Sciences section which describes a scientific study that set out to prove, using karate students, the benefits of a variety of punching training drills. Punch bag training registered 'significant increases in dynamic strength of 14% to 53%.'

Get fitter – get better

Regular training will lead to improved technical skill, starting with footwork, mobility and basic straight punches, then progressing to crosses, hooks and uppercuts, then combinations of all of them, performed in organised clusters. As your stamina improves and you reach a good level of fitness, you should experience less fatigue to interfere with concentration. Technique can then play a larger part in training: when tiredness sets in, your focus on technical aspects diminishes. It is therefore important to concentrate, at least initially, on improving your fitness in equal measure with your technique.

Preparation

Simply holding the pads can be, according to the intensity of the exercise, a workout in its own right. It is crucial that the person who is going to be hitting the pads warms up properly, but the holder should not be 'caught cold' either. The following warm-ups are tailored to the exercise which is to follow, as any warm up should be.

»   Skip rope for 3 minutes

»   Shadow box for 2 minutes

Bruce Lee used to throw 500 punches as part of his warm up; why not take it a little easier on yourself and throw just 50 punches in a relaxed fashion as part of your pre-activity rehearsal? Once this becomes insultingly easy, graduate to 100, or possibly more. Lee also trained on pads and various bags three days a week.

Warm up/cooldown

A five-minute warm-up will only raise your body heat enough to make a short stretch safe; longer, deeper stretching at this stage can lead to micro-trauma, and thus may prove to be counterproductive.

This five-minute warm-up will be adequate for most recreational exercisers; professionals will, in all likelihood, work to their own agenda. In the end it usually comes down to time management. In my experience, if people are training in their lunch hour they do not want to spend a long time warming up and stretching – they want to 'cut to the chase' and get on with the workout.

The workout should be concluded with a warm-down, following the same time and form as the warm-up: skip 3 minutes, shadow box 2 minutes.

The last stage of the workout should be a cool-down stretch, with stretches held for 10-30 seconds for each body part.

(See "Stretching," Chapter 9).

Working on focus pads

2. How to hold the pads

Everybody has some idea how to hit a punch bag. It's just hanging there, looking at you and asking to be belted. Good technique will invariably give greater satisfaction, but just pounding a bag any old how still gives immense stress relief to many, in my experience.

Not a great many people are instructed in the correct procedure for focus pad holding; after a few aches and strains later they may well wish they had been. The following text hopes to advise you on how to hold pads without injury and, at the same time, provide maximum benefit to the person you will be holding the pads for.

Preventing pains and strains

Learning to hold pads properly is essential to prevent elbow ligament injuries, such as the dreaded 'tennis elbow' which affects the common extensor tendon of the elbow, or its partner-in-crime, 'golfer's elbow', which affects the common flexor tendon. Both these injuries can be incurred without ever lifting a racquet or club; both are equally painful and debilitating.

Left: Tennis Elbow

Below: Golfer's Elbow

In order to prevent strains and overuse injuries, the following **specific** stretches should precede a session of pad holding, as in the pictures below. Follow with wrist circling and finger shaking.

The arms should stay relaxed to alleviate the 'shock' factor; the holder must learn to anticipate blows and absorb the energy in a technique similar to fielding a cricket ball or baseball, by allowing a little 'give' on contact, although without weakening the hitting surface.

The pads should be carefully adjusted before use to make sure they fit snugly. Floppy pads should be avoided, and loose straps should be secured, or cropped, to prevent the risk of eye injury. A flick in the eyeball from a 'whippy' length of leather may lead to injury, and would certainly put a crimp in your workout.

Left: wrist and hand stretches.

Above: Fingers exposed

Below: Fingers enclosed safely

If you have big hands or long fingers, you will need pads large enough to accommodate the full extent of your fingers. Squeezing your hands into pads that are too small can leave your fingers open to injury.

A finger that extends to the very end of the pad can quite easily be struck on the tip (see pictures, left); as the rest of the finger is trapped in the pad this can prove extremely painful. Beginners cannot be expected to land clean punches on the centre of the pad with unerring regularity, and the errant shot could be the one that hammers the fingertip hard enough to dislocate it.

Novice punchers should, initially, merely be encouraged to use sound technique, but with advancement should come 'counters' by the holder, to remind the hitter to defend themselves at all times. A playful slap from a cushioned pad can warn of the dangers that may follow later from a sparring or competition glove. It is merely a case of being slightly cruel in order to be kind, although this tactic is inadvisable against beginners, who may not initially be able to emotionally deal with this approach.

The holder should instruct, encourage, and try to motivate the puncher, continually re-enforcing correct technique, otherwise the individual may as well practice hitting on the punch bag.

Correct holding for the following punches

Correct holding for jab/cross combination – note the pads are close enough to the head to imitate realism but not so close as to render the holder vulnerable to a "follow through" punch.

When holding for left-handers (southpaws) reverse all stances.

Left jab to head

Left jab to body

Straight right/right cross to head

Straight right to body

Left hook high (head shot)

Left hook low (body shot)

Right hook high (head shot)

Right hook low (body shot)

Right uppercut

Left uppercut

Left 'shovel' hook

Right 'shovel' hook

Right 'screwed' punch

Where a smaller/slighter person is holding the pads for a much more powerful opponent it may be advisable to employ the double pad holding technique (as shown).

IMPORTANT TIP

When holding for uppercuts *never* hold the pads directly under your chin (most people only get this wrong just the once).

3. How to move

When working on the hanging punch bag you will decide your own foot movement, adjusting only to cope with the swing of the bag; a bag that hangs from the ceiling will, of course allow 360 degree navigation, but a bag hanging from a wall bracket will limit you to 180 degrees. On focus pads it is more challenging as the holder will usually dictate what steps you will need to take. Having said that, the following instructions – the basics – apply for forward, backward and lateral movement.

Essential Movement

(Left-handers, please reverse all instructions.)

Novices will often shape up to lead with their strong hand, and are often surprised to learn that they will be required to lead with their less competent hand, unless they have the massive fortune to be totally ambidextrous, in which case they can take their pick. It should be explained why they require to adopt this stance, rather than just expect them to take it on blind faith. There are three basic reasons, in my opinion.

»   The more competent dexterity of the right hand will provide a better defence for your face than the left, so needs to be the rear hand.

»   The right hand delivers the big punch, but it needs the left to act as a range finder (or 'can opener') to provide the opportunity to be unleashed. Leading with the right hand and trying to deliver the power punch off the weaker side would be a futile exercise. The jab is initially the weaker punch, but enforcing sound technique, abetted by specific power training, can turn it into a formidable weapon.

» Try moving around, in the manner described above, with your right foot leading; it soon becomes apparent to most students the rear foot is the dominant, more powerful and more comfortable option for precise controlled boxing footwork, in addition to providing a stable stance.

You should stand as if you are on a giant clock face with your feet at 20 past 12, your lead foot (left foot for right-handers, right foot for left-handers) on 12 o'clock and the rear foot on twenty past. The toe of the lead foot points directly ahead, while the toe of the rear foot points slightly outward.

Your hips stay 'square', but your upper body should lean minimally forward towards the target zone. You are not bolt upright, but slightly crouched. Your chin is low enough to trap a tennis ball beneath your chin and your upper chest, but your eyes are up, looking at the target. Both elbows are tucked comfortably against the ribs; this is an early precaution and good habit to get into, to defend against body hooks. The right hand is semi-closed, prepared to either block an incoming jab or throw a punch. I like to compare the right hand as a wicket-keeper's glove when in its defensive position held close to the chin, but ready to be transformed into a 'housebrick' as it travels to its target.

The left hand is held at the same height as the right, but forward of it,

with about 12" between the gloves. The pose with both gloves against the face is inadvisable for beginners, as mastering this form of cover is an advanced technique. The left glove should be closed, ready to throw a jab, or semi-closed when called upon to fend off an incoming right hand punch.

The knees should have a slight bend to encourage a 'springy' feel, the arms need to feel relaxed, as should the neck — avoid any tension at all costs.

Moving Around – The Basics

All you need to remember when starting out is:

» **the front foot takes you forward**

» **the back foot takes you backwards**

» **if you want to go to the right – move the right foot and push off with the left foot in a lateral direction**

» **if you want to go to the left – move the left foot and push off with the right foot in a lateral direction**

Stay on the balls of your feet and practice maintaining good balance and form as you move forward, backward and sideways. Practice 'circling': moving clockwise and anti-clockwise is an excellent drill for beginners.

When going forward and back, 'step and slide':

» Going forward – step with the left and allow the right to slide after it, maintaining the 20 past 12 stance.

» Going backwards — step back with the right foot and slide the left foot backwards to follow it. The 'slide' should follow the 'step' in rapid succession. Practice should very soon allow you to perfect this simple manoeuvre.

Bouncing around is labour-intensive, impractical and not good to look at (glance in the mirror if you don't believe me); instead, move around in an energy-conserving, smooth sliding motion. Attempt to glide around like a ballroom dancer — a tough ballroom dancer.

Breathing

Breathe in through the nose; if at a later, more advanced stage you want to get used to using a gumshield, this is a necessity. If you intend to progress to sparring you will most certainly require a gumshield, which will require you to keep your mouth closed — being struck on the lower jaw with the mouth open can be calamitous. To get used to this 'nose only' inhalation technique, don't wait until you are actually sparring — get into the habit while working on focus pads. Regulating your breathing is important; both to pace yourself and to stay relaxed, thus avoiding tension, a vital consideration. Inhaling through the nose is roughly three times more effective than through the mouth — so don't be a 'mouth-breather'.

'a good Western boxer hits from every angle. Each punch sets him in a position to deliver another punch. He is always on centre, never off balance...for until balance is gained, a man is ineffective in both attack and defence.'

Bruce Lee (from 'Jeet Kune Do')

Balance

Good balance is crucial as poor balance will result in poor performance. The correct stance, with arms and legs relaxed, shoulders maintained over the hips, will be a good base to work from, but self-help involving core training to strengthen and develop the stabilising muscles can help enormously.

4. How to hit

The punches for pads and bags are obviously the same. The only variation is that, on the punch bag, the hitter determines which punch to throw, whereas on the focus pads it will be the holder's positioning of the pads or verbal instruction that will determine which punch is required.

Anybody intending to spend time training on focus pads or punch bags would be well advised to wrap their hands. For the princely sum of around £3–5 you can prevent hand and wrist injury and the likelihood of delayed pain quite easily. Any responsible trainer should encourage the use of wraps, especially with regard to novice punchers, particularly when working the heavier bags.

[See chapter 10 "Equipment", for information on buying wraps.]

Whether you are hitting the pads, the bag or sparring it is wise to protect your hands and wrist, which is particularly prone to injury in beginners.

Inexperienced hitters have a tendency to cock their wrist in what I have, fairly accurately, heard described as a "swan neck" fashion, which is highly likely to prove damaging to the wrist, most likely in the form of a strain or a mild sprain. If wrist pain is felt then training should cease immediately and ice applied as a precautionary measure. Wearing wraps supports the wrist joint as well as the vulnerable small bones of the hand; it also encourages a 'flat' wrist action on striking, the wrap applying a firm bond between hand and wrist to form a strong solid unit. Should niggling wrist pain continue, consider continuing your wrapping further up the arm.

There are various ways of wrapping. The example I have given is one commonly used at our gym, but there are numerous variations and you may, in time, develop a system of wrapping best suited to your individual need. A lot will depend on the length of your wraps; you want to protect your hand but still manage to get a glove on without using a shoehorn. An investment in wraps is a wise one; hand and wrist injuries are, unfortunately, quite common and can sideline you for a frustratingly long period.

Cautionary note; wash your wraps frequently, as your hands sweat profusely when wrapped up and encased in boxing gloves. Repeated use of wraps without washing can give the impression that they could crawl away on their own.

Making a Fist

Many beginners are unsure of the way to make a "fist" in the correct fashion in order to prevent injuring the hand, especially the thumb. Most injuries beginners incur are to the wrist, usually through failure to keep the arm straight when landing the punch, or to the thumb, usually due to incorrect positioning of the thumb on contact.

The following guide is for the benefit of the absolute novice;

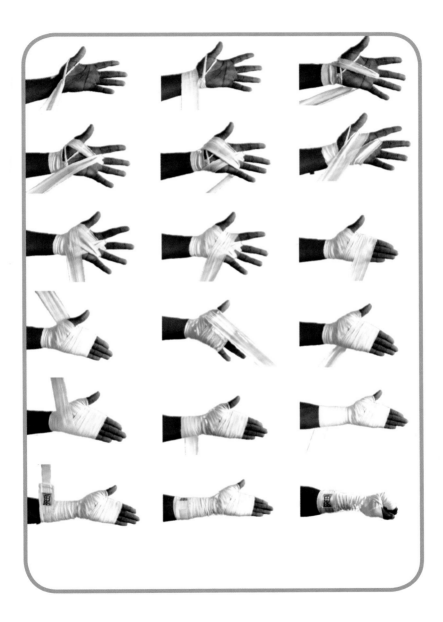

» Settle the hand comfortably into the glove, pulling hard on the wristband to ensure a snug fit. When buying gloves remember to allow enough room in them for handwraps. Your hand may expand slightly during training, so never buy tight-fitting gloves; it is generally advisable to own your own gloves, (quite apart from the 'bouquet' issue).

» Close the hand, leaving the thumb in the "thumbs up" position. Then close the bent thumb tightly down against the fingers (see illustrations below).

The thumb *must* be retained in this position when striking; failure to do so will almost certainly lead to injury.

» If retaining the thumb in this fashion (there is no alternative) proves difficult, consider thumbless gloves or cropping the thumbs of your current gloves. As in the case of footwear, never persist with kit that is uncomfortable. The problem is unlikely to improve with wear, in actual fact it is more likely to deteriorate.

Relax!

Beginners, not surprisingly, often feel tense when they start hitting something hard. Every effort should be made to encourage a relaxed approach as loose limbs travel faster. Tension can ruin technique and gives no added power or force.

Good breathing technique helps to create a relaxed approach and eliminates anxiety and fatigue.

Punches

The Jab

The jab is the first punch the novice has to master, and its importance cannot be overstated. It is the most dependable weapon for initiating an attack and is an effective form of defence. It is thrown from a safe defensive stance, limiting the degree of risk taken; it can be quite easily 'doubled' or 'trebled' for added effect.

It is essential (as in all punches) to make firm contact with the knuckle part of the glove, ensuring only the large knuckles of the hand are employed. The hand contains too many brittle bones to hit with anything other than this solid area.

The jab acts like a spear, thrust sharply towards the target. It should always be delivered crisply and cleanly at the target. A half-hearted effort can invite a dangerous counter from a right cross. Take the shortest and most direct route to the target – in other words, a straight line.

» Push off powerfully from the rear foot (you must raise the heel) to ensure a transfer of weight forward from the 'passive' to the 'active' mode. Consider the ball of the rear foot to be the starting point – the small spark that starts the big fire.

» Turn the hip in the direction of the punch-line, which will ensure the weight of the backside gets involved. 'Arm-only' punches are totally ineffective – learn to punch your weight by getting a good hip turn as you deliver the punch. Punch 'through' the pad to get in the habit of hitting hard, don't aim merely to reach the pad – try, in your mind's eye, to blast a hole right through the pad.

» As you make contact it is important to move your head 'off-line'. If you get in the habit of allowing your head to stay in the same place when you jab you will become vulnerable to a counter punch. Move your head and shoulders minimally to your right – away from what would be your opponent's right hand. Retract the hand instantly on the line it travelled out along, while maintaining your right hand in a defensive position alongside your jaw. Keep both hands up at all times – think defensively.

The Straight Right/ Right Cross

Time to unleash the beast, one of the most satisfying and pleasurable sensations known to mankind – belting an inanimate object with all the might and main of your 'big' hand. Resist the temptation to hit wildly, or 'follow through', Rocky-style. Control is essential to sound technique. This needs to be a piston-like action, delivered dynamically from a solid base, and, as with the jab, retracted instantly after completion, regardless of the effectiveness of the delivery.

» Drive off the ball of the rear foot; the more power you muster will be reflected in the strength and speed of your punch. Speed cannot be underestimated: a slow, ponderous or lazy effort is hardly likely to be effective. 'Snap' in all punches is an essential ingredient; it allows lightweights to throw a punch that is more effective than that thrown by some heavyweights, due to the shock value.

» This being a hard punch, it is mandatory to use the hardest part of the hand, the top row of knuckles, delivered with a slightly downward action to ensure the knuckle area alone makes solid contact. Turn the right hip and shoulder powerfully in the direction of the blow to ensure your full weight gets behind the punch. As this punch is of a higher risk tariff than the jab you wouldn't want to waste it.

» Keep the shoulders over the hips, don't stretch to reach the target, move the whole body forward as a unit, taking a small step with the left foot if necessary to ensure your backside is moving forward. Don't leave your power behind.

Shut that Door

Both the jab and cross can be likened to the action of a slamming door. When throwing the jab the right side acts as a solid base, like the hinged side of the door, allowing the left side to swing forward. When the forceful right hand punch is thrown the roles are reversed and the left side acts as a hinge while the right side slams forward, hopefully akin to an outhouse door in a force nine gale. Allowing any movement by the stabilising side interferes with the overall dynamic.

DON'T JUST PUNCH *TO* IT – PUNCH *THROUGH* IT!

As mentioned above don't punch to merely reach the intended target, punch 'through it' as if you are going to knock a hole in it; this will get you hitting harder and get you used to the idea that opponents have a habit of backing up when they see a punch coming.

The Hook

The hook is usually a little harder for beginners to master, which is usually due to over-complication; it really is a relatively simple punch to learn, best thrown in a natural fashion and not over-stylised, which can reduce effectiveness.

The left hook is more commonly used than the right. It is nearer the target and thus arrives with less notice of its engagement than a right hook, thrown from further back, would. I apologise if this seems self-evident, but I was always under the impression Henry Cooper must be left-handed because he always had such a tremendous left hook, like the one that floored Mohammed Ali. Anyone who wants to know what a perfect left hook looks like should watch the film of their encounter, and note the *speed* at which the hook was thrown, as well as the perfect and powerful hooks Joe Frazier employed in his first encounter with Ali.

The left hook is used to mount a lateral attack and penetrate the defence of an opponent's protective right hand, or to counter against a right hand punch by hitting over or under the right hand. The right hook is more commonly used to follow-up a left hook or as a body punch having 'slipped' a left jab.

Basic steps are;

» Shift your weight to the side you intend to launch the hook from, slightly turning the hip and shoulder away. Slide the back foot in so that the feet are now in a quarter past twelve position, the narrower base will allow a more dynamic turn to create power, as well as making the manoeuvre simpler.

» The arm should be bent at the elbow (see variations below) at about 90 degrees. The other hand is pulled close to the head, on defensive duty.

» Raise the left heel vigorously and pivot the left hip simultaneously and make a violent (no point in mincing words here) turn and slam the left

hand against the target with the upper knuckles leading and the thumb (tucked in tightly) on top at as you make contact. The instant after delivering the hook, whip the hand back to the original defensive position.

Variations on a Hooking Theme

The shape of the arm will have much to do with the amount of power applied when throwing the hook.

» If the arm bent at the elbow forms a right angle, this will encourage a strong hip turn, which will mean greater punching power

» If the arm is at an 'obtuse angle' – greater than a right angle – there will be reduced power, as there is less hip turn.

» When the arm is at an 'acute angle', with the fist closer to the body, a full, forceful hip turn needs to be applied to register a punch with the arm in this form, resulting in an extremely strong impact from very close range.

For all three varieties of hook the feet should be at a 'quarter past twelve'.

The Shovel Hook

The shovel hook is a short-range punch to be employed when in close proximity to an opponent; ignoring the anti-social aspect, think of it as 'fighting in a phone box'. The back foot needs to slide forward into a 'quarter past twelve' position, making it easier to thrust the hips forward for maximum effect.

It is often referred to as a 'body uppercut', and is, in effect, a modified version of the uppercut, but with the arm being rammed forward at a 45 degree plane instead of the vertical, as in the uppercut. The non-hitting arm is held in close proximity to the body to protect against a counter to head or body. As with the hook and uppercut it is important to raise the heel.

The Uppercut

The uppercut is strictly a close range punch, usually delivered with the stronger hand. The following relates to a right uppercut. Basic steps are;

» Feet should, ideally, be in a 'quarter past twelve' stance.

» Drop the right shoulder below the intended target area, then drive upwards explosively with the hips as you punch upward in an almost vertical plane, a powerful push-off from the right heel allows the hips to travel upward forcefully.

» The defending hand is pulled in close to the head to guard against a counter. The palm of the hitting hand should be facing you.

» The punch should not travel much more than 12" and the hand should instantly return to 'the guard' position following delivery.

» Do not, when working on the pads, feel tempted to 'follow through' skyward, this will leave your head unguarded, a bad habit to get into.

Jabs and Crosses to the Body

A slightly different technique is employed when throwing jabs and straight rights/crosses to the body. The hitter should bend at the knees but not lean forward as this will lead to a loss of power and increase vulnerability to a counter. Try to keep the shoulders over the hips.

TIP!

There are three basic "H" related memos to remember regarding the preceding punches:

» Hands up
» Hips up
» Heels up

The left jab to the body

With the right hand defending the head, bend the knees, keeping the shoulders over the hips, gaining drive from the ball of the left foot acting as a spring as the left arm is speared at the target *fully extended* – using the full extent of the reach is important in this shot. The left hip and shoulder should follow the direction of the punch.

The Straight Right to the body

As with the jab, bend at the knees, keeping the shoulders over the hips as much as possible, the left hand defending the head. Again, the power is drawn by driving forcefully off the ball of the rear foot, turning the right hip and shoulder to follow the direction of the blow. The arm should be fully extended to achieve maximum force.

With both punches use an 'in and out' fast action, this bent knee position is not one to be caught in against a sharp counter.

Right 'screwed' punch

This punch is fired straight from the chest, the palm facing upward. Power is derived from a forceful drive of the hips and a dynamic push-off from the ball of the rear foot. The idea when using this punch is usually to attempt to drive it between the defending gloves using the element of surprise.

In addition to the above punches there is a useful ploy, particularly for anybody considering progressing to sparring, that of 'feinting', also known as 'faking' or the popular boxing term – 'kidding'. It is purely and simply a matter of pretending to throw a punch to dupe an opponent, best employed with pad-holders to gauge how canny you are at this ploy in misleading them before attempting it against an actual sparring partner – one of the advantages pads have over punch bags, which is why training should, ideally, include both.

Note: in the chapter on combination punching it is referred to as 'faking'. Why? 'Feinting' sounds too much like lapsing into unconsciousness, and 'kidding' sounds a little too crude, whereas 'faking' implies an element of artfulness, as is hoped to be achieved in this ploy.

5. How to Defend

I cannot help but feel it would be negligent to instruct somebody how to hit, yet fail to inform him or her what action to take when or if somebody used these blows against them. In boxing an action begets a reaction. Hopefully the following will help to arm you with, or at least inform you of, the required defensive actions to take.

Always bear in mind that if you and the incoming punch are travelling in the same direction at the same time the impact is lessened enormously; avoid 'head on' collisions, they can have disastrous results.

Defence Against The Jab

The rear hand should be in close proximity to the face, making a small circular movement in readiness for action. Block the incoming lead with the semi-clenched rear glove, 'fielding' it to deflect it away from your head, not slapping it away, excessive travel by your rear hand could leave your head exposed to a follow up hook-off-the-jab shot. Wait until the jab has passed your own lead hand before getting involved, going out to meet the anticipated blow will leave a large gap, again rendering you vulnerable to a follow-up hook.

Defence Against The Straight Right

The lead hand, with which an opponent will jab, is close to you and needs quick reactions, but the rear hand is far enough back for you to get

a little more notice of its approach. For this reason your defence is three-fold.

» Steer the incoming right hand away with your left hand

» Turn your shoulder, tucking your chin in order to glance over the shoulder, your right hand in front of the lower half of your face, the arm across your chest. The blow will land on your shoulder blade and will be nullified if you pull back at the same time.

» Simply move backward as the blow is arriving to let it fall short of its target.

The Hook

I have chosen three of these techniques (hopefully the most useable).

The Head Hook

» Raise the arm to block the blow, taking it on or around the elbow. This is the most reliable form of defence against close range hooks. Some

consider that the left hook is the most dangerous punch to defend against, as it comes around fast from out of the line of vision and subsequently is often seen very late – too late for some people!

»   'Bob and Weave'. This is inadvisable against a much shorter opponent. As you become aware of the hook arriving, bend at the knees, keeping your head and shoulders above your hips, *do not bend forward excessively at the waist,* your hands and arms tucked in, although a crisp shot to your opponents body from the 'bob' position is the ideal bonus. Come up after the blow has, hopefully, sailed over your head, moving slightly to the side from which the punch came – think of the move as 'down and out'.

» 'Swayback/Snapback'. This is the best ploy for anybody who is considerably taller than their opponent; simply sway back to avoid the swing of the arm, ready to sway back to the more vertical stance in order to be in position to counter.

Defence against body shots

The general defence to employ against most body attacks is to move backward or sideways in the same direction the punch arrives in, thereby lessening the impact, using your arms held closely in front of your body to nullify any impression on your body.

With body hooks, ensure your elbows are tucked tightly against your ribs in order to absorb a lateral attack. Make sure you are moving away from the impact at the same time for complete damage limitation. See

'Technique Drills – Glove under arm drill'.

Do not try to slap away a body shot; you may end up directing the punch to a different area of your anatomy, a delicate one at that.

'Slipping'

Using lateral movement to avoid an incoming punch is referred to as 'slipping', pulling the head off-line by reacting sharply while, if possible, throwing a counterpunch. This technique requires a great deal of practice to gain confidence, as the margin for error is slender.

Mind your head – move your head

It should be remembered when considering defence how important it is to constantly move your head. An opponent, even with your glove in his face, still has a pretty accurate idea of where your head is – at the other end of your arm, you don't need to be an anatomist to work it out. The answer, therefore, is to move your head and shoulders every time you throw a punch, as you move around, or as you fake to throw a punch. Simply move from the waist, shifting the head and shoulders in small, smooth movements. The moving target, as everybody knows, is the hardest to hit; ensure you are hard to hit by keeping your head and shoulders moving.

6. Fifty Combinations

In this chapter, the punches are shown performed on focus pads, but exactly the same technique applies to punch bag training. It is fairly obvious that the increased demands of focus pad work renders it a more advanced form of training, whereas the heavy bag is necessary to build up dynamic power for hard punching. The lighter bags are essential for speed of reaction and fast-punching technique.

Where the combination requires focus pads I have listed them, but many of these can be modified or abridged to suit punch bag training.

Once more, apologies to left-handers, kindly reverse all instructions.

Unless stated, punches are head height; when head and body punches are combined each will be stipulated.

1. Multiple Jabs

The very simplest combination is putting more than one jab together. It is a useful manoeuvre, as the first jab can be used as a 'range finder'. The second jab should follow the first in rapid succession, with no reduction in speed, power or correct technique.

2. Jab and straight right/cross

Why start with the left and not the right? The answer is that as the right hand is coming from as far back as your head, your opponent sees it coming and has ample time for avoidance; it needs the left to act as a foil to set it up.

The true 'right cross' refers to a right hand punch thrown over or under a left lead, a perfect counter punch, as it would catch the opponent coming in, multiplying the weight of the punch. An analogy is when two cars collide head-on. As opposed to shunting the other car travelling in the same direction, the result is that usually double the weight of the blow is incurred.

The important point in this combination is to maintain maximum power, but ensure the left comes back rapidly to protect the head the instant the right is thrown. The head should not remain undefended at any stage of the move.

3. Left jab, straight right /cross, left hook, right hook

The jab and cross are thrown from the 'twenty past twelve' stance, but for the hooks the back foot should slide in to 'quarter past twelve'.

4. Double left jab, straight right/cross, left hook

5. Left hook to body, left hook to head, right uppercut

6. Left jab, straight right/cross, left hook to head, right uppercut, left hook to head.

7. Left jab, straight right/cross, left uppercut, right uppercut.

8. Left jab to head, straight right to body, left hook to head, straight right to head

9. Left hook to head, right hook to body, left hook to body, right hook to head

10. Jab to head, jab to body, jab to head, straight right/cross

11. Double jab coming forward, double jab backing up from holder (focus pads)

12. Jabbing either pad, high and low, single and double (focus pads)

13. Throwing a 'hook off the jab' combination.

In this technique the left jab is thrown normally, but the left arm is only half retracted to then throw a left hook.

14. 'Hook off the jab, followed by straight right/cross, left hook.

15. Left jab, straight right/cross,
bob and weave from hook thrown by holder (focus pads)

Hooks can be thrown from both hands, according to which is executed more easily first.

16. Block left jab thrown by holder while responding with own jab

17. As above, follow with straight right/cross, left hook (focus pads)

18. Block incoming left jab, deflect incoming straight right, both thrown by holder, counter with own left jab and straight right (focus pads)

19. As above, followed by left hook, right hook (focus pads)

20. Left jab, screwed right hand, left hook, right uppercut.

21. Block left and right body hooks, counter with high/head left and right hooks (focus pads)

22. Block left and right head hooks, counter with left and right body hooks

23. Move pad around for all punches

Providing a moving target increases the degree of difficulty. This is an advanced drill for the more experienced hitter, and the punches should be not thrown with full force for safety reasons.

24. Slap & Turn

Initially the hitter faces away from the holder. Following a slap on the back, the hitter spins around, having to react to whatever punches the pads are held for. The position of the pads should be changed on each repetition.

25. Hiding the pads

Holder keeps the pads behind his back, then produces them smartly, giving the hitter only a brief time for rapid response.

26. 'Slip' a left jab from the holder's pad by stepping to the left while simultaneously throwing a right cross

Follow up with a left hook and a right uppercut.

Slipping jab with right cross.

27. Hitter dictates

The holder puts the pads up but does not know when the hitter will strike, or from which hand. This is a useful drill for learning to fake, by seeing if the hitter can dupe the holder.

28. Double jab, right shovel hook, left and right hooks

Right shovel hook

29. "Freestyle Mode"

Holder simply offers the pad, without verbal instruction, for the hitter to strike; with each pad offered the range of punches should include everything in the individual hitter's repertoire.

30. Left jab, left uppercut, right cross, left hook, right hook

Left uppercut.

31. Left jab, bob and weave from hook, left hook, right cross, left hook (focus pads)

32. Left jab, double bob and weave (from left and right hooks), right cross, left hook, right cross (focus pads)

Bob & weave from left and right hooks

33. Left jab, left hook, left hook, right cross

34. Left jab, right cross, left hook, right cross

35. Left jab, left uppercut, right cross, right cross, left hook, right cross

36. Left jab, right uppercut, left hook, slip left jab, right cross (focus pads)

The right uppercut

37. 'Fake' with jab but throw right cross, left hook, bob and weave, left hook, right cross, left hook

38. Left hook, right cross, left hook, double bob and weave (from 2 x hooks), left hook, right cross, left hook.

39. Defend against left hook, (cover up or 'snap back'), left hook, right cross, left hook. (focus pads)

40. Defend against left hook (cover up or 'snap back'), left hook, bob and weave, right cross, left hook, right uppercut. (focus pads)

Cover up

41. Defend against right hook (cover up or 'snap back'), left hook, right cross, left hook, right cross (focus pads)

42. Defend against right hook (cover up or 'snap back'), right cross, bob and weave, right cross, left hook, right cross (focus pads)

43. Left jab, right cross, defend against right hook (cover up or 'snap back'), right cross, left hook, right hook (focus pads)

44. Left jab, right cross, defend against right hook (cover up or 'snap back'), right cross, double bob and weave, left hook, right cross, left hook

45. Left jab, right cross, left hook, defend against left hook (cover up or 'snap back'), left hook, right cross, left hook (focus pads)

46. 'Fake' left jab, right cross, left hook head, left hook body, bob and weave, left hook head, right uppercut (focus pads)

47. Block left jab, block right hook right cross, bob and weave, left jab, right cross to body, left hook, right cross to head (focus pads)

48. Double left jab, bob and weave, left jab, left uppercut, right cross, left hook, right cross (focus pads)

Bob and weave

49. 'Slip' left jab while simultaneously throwing right cross, left hook, bob and weave, right shovel hook, left hook, right cross (focus pads)

Right: Slipping jab. Opposite: slipping cross.

50. Left jab to head, right cross to body, left hook to head, left hook to body, left hook to head, right uppercut.

7. Technique drills

The following drills are intended simply to re-enforce sound technique.

Jab over arm drill

(focus pads)

The holder holds up one pad to be hit, and uses the other to form a right angle, just below it. In order to punch cleanly and retract the arm correctly, the hand must travel along the correct plane both forward and backward.

Glove under arm drill

(focus pads or punch bags)

While jabbing with the left the hitter must retain a glove under the arm. This re-enforces the need to keep the elbow of the defending arm tucked tightly against the ribs to defend against blows to this area. The lead arm punches can progress to hooks and uppercuts, but the glove must be retained (on penalty of press-ups or similar exercise, or payment of post training refreshments!)

Circling Footwork Drill

(focus pads)

Place a focus pad or an object of similar size, i.e. a pair of gloves, on the floor. Both the holder and the hitter circle around the pad, facing each other whilst moving left and right. When the holder stops moving the hitter throws punches in response to position of pads. The holder instigates all movement.

Footwork Speed Drill

(focus pads)

For this drill a reasonable amount of space is required (a boxing ring is between 14–20 square feet). The holder moves rapidly around the area, pausing without notice to hold the pads up to be struck; the hitter's role is to chase him down, always 'in his space', ready to throw fast punches before the holder sets off again. It goes without saying the holder needs to be in reasonable shape to conduct this drill.

Long and Short/Short and Long (Footwork & Jab Drill)

(focus pads)

Holder extends one pad toward the hitter, the other in front of his shoulder. The hitter will jab the nearest pad, then by adjusting footwork, progress immediately to hit the pad furthest away. The drill is then changed, whereby the hitter now strikes the pad furthest away first, then backs up to jab the other pad.

Tennis Ball Drill

(focus pads and punch bags)

In order to instil correct head positioning – chin down, eyes up – hitter retains a tennis ball under the chin while training on the focus pads. Small participants can use a golf ball, should the tennis ball prove too bulky.

Slap and Turn

(focus pads)

A drill to speed up reaction time, by testing the hitter's responses. The hitter faces away from the holder, who is positioned an arm's length behind him/her. The holder slaps the hitter on the back, at which signal he/she is required to spin around rapidly and respond to the angle of the proffered pads as to whether to jab, cross, hook etc. If performed fast enough for enough 2-3 minute rounds this can also be considered a fitness drill.

Hide the Pads

(focus pads)

Another reaction drill; the pad-holder moves around with the pads concealed behind the back, then produces them abruptly to draw an instant response from the hitter.

Light Bag Bob and Weave

(punch bag)

You will need a bag that is about 3' in length and not too heavy for this drill. Throw a few hooks to get the bag swinging laterally, then bob and weave under the bag, coming up to throw more hooks.

Slipping the Bag

(punch bag)

Throw a few straight punches to get the bag swinging to and fro, then let it slip past you on its approach. When it loses its momentum start over again.

8. Fitness drills

Punching curl-ups

(focus pads only)

Hitter is in position to perform curl-ups, lying on the floor with knees bent at a right angle. The holder stands over the hitter, offering the pads up to be punched. The pads are slowly retracted, forcing the hitter to curl the upper body forward to make contact. In this manner the holder produces up and down motion, making it challenging work for the abdominal muscles.

Stamina Drill

(**preferably on focus pads:** having somebody else determine what punches are required greatly enhances the degree of difficulty and, in doing so, demands greater stamina and reactionary skill).

Using a timer the hitter is required to work continuously in "freestyle mode" (drill number 29 in the Combinations chapter), for a predetermined time. Novices should begin at around 30 seconds, building up until capable of hitting for 3-minute rounds. For the latter a 30 second rest between rounds is advisable; gradually build up stamina by increasing the number of rounds.

Endurance Drill

(**focus pads or punch bags**)

As above but consisting of 3-6 rounds of one minute's duration. Round 1 = easy, Round 2 = faster & harder hitting Round 3 = fast and hard. This sequence can then be repeated.

Crunch and Punch

(**focus pads or punch bags**)

Hitter throws 10 punches, drops to floor to perform 10 crunches, jumping up to repeat the action. Sequence should continue for an agreed set of repetitions or predetermined time span, usually 1-2 minutes.

This drill can be utilised for various exercises or a medley of exercises, substituting such callisthenics as curl-ups, reverse curls, body-weight squats, squat thrusts, press/push-ups, rotational push-ups, burpees, star jumps, tuck jumps, body-weight forward lunges and reverse lunges, tricep dips and back extensions.

"Shuttle" Punching

(focus pads or punch bag)

Best performed in a hall with ample space, or outdoors. The hitter throws ten punches, then sets off on a sprinting shuttle run for 4-5 yards, returns and repeats the sequence continuously. Decide on number of repetitions or time span prior to commencement.

"Punch the Clock" – 2 x drills

(focus pads or punch bag)

» How fast can you throw 100 punches (any combination)? If on the focus pads the holder calls the punch count and needs to keep the clock in sight, or, better still, the timer within earshot. To improve endurance increase the number of punches in multiples of 20. If on the punch bag you'll need to do your own count and use a timer (see timers), or use a bag where you can see the wall clock.

» How many punches can you get off in one, two or three minutes? The holder counts the punches; if on the punch bag all you need is a timer loud enough to be audible above the sound of your wheezing/gasping.

The Hundred Punch Drill

(focus pads or punch bag)

An endurance drill; start with;

50 (in total) jabs and crosses, i.e. jab, cross, jab, cross etc.

50 hooks, i.e. left hook, right hook, left hook, right hook etc.

30 second rest – and start again; do as many 100's as you can manage.

If on focus pads the holder counts (loudly).

Punchbag Thrust

(heavy punch bag, preferably)

A plyometric drill wherein the punch bag is pushed away with a vigorous shoulder turn, and its return is abruptly arrested using the same hand. Try the following, while adopting your natural boxing stance.

10 push and stop with the left hand only

10 push and stop with the right hand only

10 push and stop with both hands

It is hard to find plyometric training for boxing and I feel this is the only specific one I have come across

Make sure the coast is clear before launching into your 'shove and shock' routine and no unsuspecting bystanders are in range or you may be called upon to implement your defensive skills (or find a new gym).

9. Stretching

Pre activity stretching

All that is required after a 5 minute warm up is a short stretch, (taking just over a minute).

Sequence

These stretches should each take **6-8 seconds**

Shoulder stretch,

Back (standing)

Chest

Obliques

Hamstrings (standing)

Quads (standing)

Hip Flexors

Calf

Soleus and Achilles

Triceps

Neck

Post Activity Stretching

If the workout has been hard, and time allows, each body part can be stretched for 30 seconds each. At the very least the short stretch should be repeated, holding each stretch a little longer, time allowing. If it is possible include the following stretches to your warm down;

Back Stretch

Lower back stretch

Glutes

Quads

Adductors

10. Equipment required

Bag Gloves/Mitts

When it comes to these training gloves you are usually faced with a choice of buying your own, costing between around £10 – £60, according to quality, material or brand name.

Always go for good quality leather gloves; vinyl gloves are cheaper, but poor in quality, (leather lets the hands 'breathe'), offer limited protection for the hands, apart from a tendency to split easily and, after a few wears, smell like a cat that expired last week. Even top of the range leather gloves can get a little "high" after a long period of use. This should be easily rectified with treatment by Dettol, or a similar anti-bacterial surface cleaner – all the main supermarkets have their own brands and are equally remedial. One squirt into the glove on a regular basis should remove offensive odours.

Try to always use your own gloves; some gyms have a 'lucky dip' box from which anybody who does not possess their own gloves can select a pair; needless to say these can leave your hands with a fetid fragrance no soap known to mankind can neutralise for days – get your own gloves if you are going to train regularly on pads or punch bags. If your gloves fail to respond to anti-bacterial treatment, you should assume they have started to grow their own culture internally, and discard them.

Good gloves come in small, medium and large, so always 'try before you buy'; for reasons of allowing for wraps and possible hand expansion once your hands get hot, which they inevitably will during a workout. You should never buy tight-fitting gloves, any more than you should buy tight-fitting running shoes, for the same reason: possible heat expansion. Once you are happy with your gloves, reel back the years to your schooldays, and write your name/initials on them, for that occasion when you leave the gym tired and confused by your exertions and leave your gloves behind. Phoning to report them missing with the only available description being "they are red" will not help those seeking them, especially at a boxing/martial arts establishment, where there are inevitably a pile of forsaken gloves.

If you find you are having problems with the thumb, (for some unfathomable reason many manufacturers invariably endow every glove with 'large' size on the thumb), one solution may be a pair of 'thumbless gloves" (Twins sell these for £25), or simply prune the thumb of your own gloves. Whichever solution you prefer, strive to ensure your thumb is 'tucked in'. See "making a fist" p.42.

If you have delicate or vulnerable hands, or are concerned because your hands are vital to your profession, e.g. concert pianist, hairdresser (I've experienced this twice), or if you are arthritic, I would advise wearing sparring gloves –12, 14 or 16 oz – to give your hands a great deal of padding to protect them. For the same reason you will need well-padded focus pads if you intend to do any holding. Personally I would recommend the curved Title pads for this instance, as they are extremely thick and substantial enough to give solid protection against the most vigorous hitting. A brand called Gelshock produce bag gloves internally padded with a gel and foam combination (also focus pads of a similar construction, see below), to minimize impact and claim to "provide superior hand protection", unfortunately I have only seen them advertised on an American website, www.ringside.com, at a cost of $45.

Handwraps

Wraps will lessen any abrasion from your gloves, as well as protecting the small bones of the hands and prevent the wrist being 'cocked' and thereby prone to injury.

The most user-friendly variety is elasticised with Velcro fastening, which keeps them in position. The plain linen variety has a tendency to be become unravelled and baggy. Give your wraps a (frequent) good wash with a little fabric softener added and they will last for years. Expect to pay around £5 for your wraps, but I have seen them in major chain stores for under £3 (non-elasticised Lonsdale variety).

TIP

If your handwraps are incredibly long (many are, as long wraps suit the big-handed type),put them on and work out how much material you have over once you have wrapped your hand to your satisfaction. Cut from the middle of the wrap the exact length you found to be surplus and simply sew them back together – it doesn't matter how good or bad your stitching is, who's going to see it, it merely needs to hold together. Your wraps are now 'tailor made'.

Pro-Box sell 'punch bag mitt inners', which are cotton gloves to wear inside your boxing mitts, for £4.50, but I feel wraps are superior as they can be 'tailor-made' to fit snugly.

Focus Pads/Hook and Jab Pads

If you are buying your own pads, again I would advocate buying good quality leather ones. The vinyl varieties are invariably substandard, and the canvas pads have very little 'feedback' potential. Pads can be flat or curved, depending on which variety the trainer prefers. When buying your pads consider also the people who will be punching them, I have encountered focus pads, not always cheap ones, that resemble a kerbstone when making contact with them; unfortunately some pads are just **too** hard, and may lead to you having difficulty retaining training partners. Some pads have buckles and straps, but these are rapidly being replaced with Velcro fastening, which is less fussy to secure – if the retaining Velcro straps are excessively long (many are) simply trim them with scissors to prevent getting a painful flick in the eye. Other pads simply have a 'glove' of the 'one-size-fits-all' variety – ensure your hand is comfortable in pads of this nature before you buy them.

Focus pads with a combination filling of latex, foam and gel are available from Gelshock. As with gloves, in the interests of retention, emblazon your name/initials on your pads with a permanent marker, especially if everybody at the gym uses the same brand.

Wayne Rowlands holding the author's Twins pads with marker clearly visible. If you have just paid £50 for new pads you may be advised to copy this example.

Coaching Mitts

(also referred to as Coachspar Mitts)

The author's coaching mitts giving evidence of their long service.

Coaching mitts introduce an advanced range of technique training, in particular, that of a defensive nature.

These are a hybrid of sparring glove and focus pad. They consist of a huge generously padded sparring glove with a focus area on the palm, which is strongly reinforced to sustain impact. They enable a coach to take training to the next level and introduce an element of sparring into the training regime. The trainee now not only is required to hit the pads but also defend against incoming punches thrown by a gloved hand, albeit an extremely well-padded one. It is an ideal precursor to sparring.

As can be construed from the sad and sorry state of my own coaching mitts they take quite a battering; mine are ten years old and I paid around £35 from Pro-Box (who now retail them at around £58).

'Weighted' Bag Mitts

ProBox also produce a punchbag mitt with weights at the wrist, which can be increased/decreased in weight to suit the user. This innovation would naturally offer greater resistance, albeit purely as a training aid; the added burden would almost certainly diminish technique, but it all accords what the user is setting out to achieve. Many would believe if you boxed for a succession of two minute rounds, decreasing the weight with each successive round until all the weight has been removed, that this will improve hand speed on the last round. While I cannot, with exact science, predict this to be true, I feel there is some merit in this argument, and no harm in trying. Training with small weights, to improve hand speed once the weights have been discarded, is a standard technique I have seen used for some time in martial arts gyms.

The punch cushion

On similar lines to focus pads comes the Cleto Reyes punch cushion. This is a padded two-handled pad (looking akin to a cushion from a bar-stool) that allows the coach to offer a large range of punches to the hitter. I have seen Marco Antonio Barrera (WBC Super Featherweight Champion) working with his trainer on this piece of equipment to great effect, but I feel it requires an advanced coach to get functional training from the cushion.

Punchbags

Most of the punch bags listed earlier are available for sale if you want to install one for training at home. There are, however, some aspects of home installation that must be taken into consideration. If the bag is to hang in a garage, brick-built shed, loft or converted factory or school space all it will most likely require is a stout hook from an ironmongers, with the possible addition of a swivel hook. Some bags are sold complete with chains, some merely with 'D' rings on fabric, leaving you to source your own chains and hooks. Regardless of fittings I would always recommend buying a punch bag that has been filled by the supplier rather than one you have to fill yourself – home-filling usually has about as much success as home dentistry or tattooing, in my opinion.

Home installation considerations

» If your bag needs to go on a wall bracket it is vital to take into consideration the strength of the fittings and fixings and the density of the brick; where possible seek out professional advice from a builder or engineer. The fixings might be strong enough to take the weight of your bag, but once you apply the torque of heavy punches it will be put under a much greater stress. I have seen a bag, bracket and bricks all come out together during a heavy session due to the fact that the installer did not realise the bricks were too soft when fixing the bracket.

» Noise. Your efforts on the bag will resonate far and wide, especially if you have added a speedball, with a percussive tattoo that can be picked up in the next county. If you have very close neighbours they will be unlikely to be sympathetic with your training efforts.

» If fitting is impractical or would require the expense of getting a professional in, you may plump for a stand-alone bag. The problem here comes with the weight, as these require the base to be filled with water or sand to stabilise them, lest they travel far and wide under the weight of your assault. On a concrete floor this is not a problem, but if you live in a flat, pay heed to the strength of the floor, or if it is to stand on a wooden floor, the age and strength of your floorboards – these things are heavy.

» Storage. Before you decide to hang a bag, or install a stand-alone bag remember that this beast is unlikely to be portable, and your nearest and dearest, understanding as they may be, may consider it an unattractive household addition if constantly on view.

The above reasons all go to explain why there are nearly always inexpensive punch bags on sale in the second-hand columns of your local newspaper.

Punchbags can be reasonably inexpensive, a new vinyl bag can cost as little as £30 (at time of writing), but a top of the range Reyes or Everlast can run into three figures.

Improvisation

Shown in the photograph opposite is a wall of kick-shields, where they hang awaiting use in kick-boxing drills. If the bags are hung firmly enough it makes for a multi-use punch pad, wherein several people can train simultaneously. If there is a large class the shields provide additional targets as there are unlikely to be enough punch bags for a large group to all train on at the same time, albeit the obvious limitation that they only allow for linear movement.

D.I.Y.

(We are talking budget training here...)

While it may not measure up to a £100 Everlast bag you can still assemble your own punch bag, especially if it as temporary measure. I used to have an old army kitbag stuffed with rags that served my purpose until I could get hold of a decent bag, and I would recommend it to youngsters or anybody who is looking for a cheap and cheerful option for training. Do not be tempted to use sawdust, a mistake I made with my first effort, even George Foreman in his pomp would not have enjoyed this dense medium very much, and if hung in a damp shed or garage, (as mine was), it doesn't

take long to take on the consistency of wet sand.

Fill a kitbag, a large laundry bag or a hessian sack with rags torn into thin strips, **not** in bundles. You will probably get away with hanging it with rope, avoiding the expense of buying chains. If you don't want to have the bag swing too much, fill the base with about an inch or two of sand. If you think the bag when filled with rags is still too hard try mixing the rags with ripped-up chunks of foam rubber.

Timers

If you want to work out, or train somebody, for a specified period, you want to know when that 2 or 3 minute 'round' is over. Relying on a watch while, at the same time, wearing focus pads or boxing mitts, is impractical, and glancing up at the gym clock at a crucial time may prove painful, so use a timer. It may, if the training environment is not too noisy to use the stopwatch on your digital phone, sports watch e.g. 'G' Shock, or a heart rate monitor.

A digital kitchen timer with an audible alarm will set you back £3-5 at Woolworth, Wilkinson's or Sainsbury's; small, portable and simple to use, and, in my estimation, a bargain (I picked up an 'Ascot' timer for £1.99 at Aldi).

A boxing training time clock is the ultimate, but are usually only found when training at the gym. If you want one at home, the classy, but costly (if purely for personal use), 'Round Timer' will set you back £95, or an 'Interval Timer' retails at £75, both are available from Tao Sports (www.taosports. co.uk), although there are many sites selling these types of timers and it would be well to shop around. A professional round clock, such as the Lonsdale Gym Timer costs £350 at the time of writing.

11.Other Considerations

Footwear

Seasoned campaigners may be happy with bare feet, Thai style, or boxing boots, but I would advise novices to wear trainers with support, such as cross-trainers or running shoes, ensuring the soles are not worn down. Double-knot your laces to prevent a loose lace interrupting your workout.

Boxing boots vary in cost. I would advise finding a store where you can actually try them on first, for size and comfort considerations.

Jewellery and other extras.

If you know you are going to be working on pads or bags try to leave your rings, earrings, studs, necklaces etc. at home to reduce the risk of personal injury, loss or damage to the items. Take your watch off, secure your spectacles with a lace round the back of the head, or, better still, try to make do without them. Only wear your contact lenses if you *absolutely need* them; I have lost count of the number of times I have been forced to halt a class to search for somebody's errant lens. Tie back any loose long hair that will annoy you or interfere with your vision. Avoid the temptation to train in a baseball cap. They limit upward vision, invariably fall off and are totally superfluous. If you don't feel warm enough when you start training wear a knitted cap/ bobble hat.

Pains and Strains

As stated in "How to Hit", if you feel pain in the hands or wrist, stop training and rest, preferably with an ice pack applied to the injured site for 20 minutes.

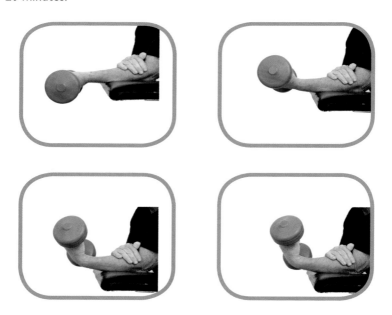

Wrist roll with undergrip

It is possible you are a newcomer to holding focus pads and your forearm muscles are taking on a repetitive challenge they have never previously encountered. If you have suffered a strain and have to take a short time off from working on the pads, try to build up the strength in your forearm in the interim period. Get a squash ball, or a 'squeezy' foam ball (they are usually in the shape of a rugby ball), and make it your constant companion, squeezing it while sitting about or watching television etc. You can also do wrist roll exercises, using light dumbbells or even soup cans, every other day (take a day off for recovery). A combination of both these strengthening practices will almost certainly give you newly acquired strength in this region.

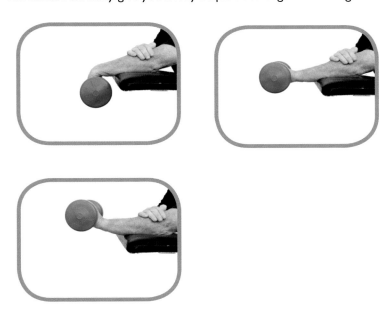

Wrist rolls with overgrip

N.B. If you feel any pain while training on bags or pads, especially in the chest – **stop training immediately**. Never forget that this is an extremely vigorous and labour-intensive form of training, you should always err on the side of caution. On the same note, if you are, or have recently been feeling unwell, resist the urge to train; rest and recover first, your training will be so much more enjoyable and beneficial once you are 100 %.

Rest!

Once many people get started on a new and absorbing way of training it is not unusual to find they cannot get enough of it, and there can be a tendency to hurl themselves into workouts with an almost religious zeal. A lot of beginners inform me that, although they love working on punch bags and pads, "my hand/arm/wrist aches/hurts/is killing me".

Like all forms of training, rest and recovery is essential to allow for adaptation and improvements to develop, and working on focus pads is particularly stressful to the newcomer's wrist, hand and arm muscles, especially if they have never indulged in this form of training before. My advice is, if there is any hint of pain or soreness, to take some time out until it feels right. Functional or specific exercises such as shadow boxing or skipping should help you with co-ordination, and keep you sharp for your 'comeback'.

No sweat

It is inevitable that training of this nature is liable to cause a copious amount of perspiring. While this natural coolant – sweat – tells you that you are putting some effort into your workout it is no fun when the sweat runs into your eyes with the effect of making them sting. Avoid this unnecessary and unpleasant hindrance by smearing a little petroleum jelly/Vaseline along the most protuberant part of the eye socket, usually the eyebrow line. The sweat dripping from your head and brow should now cascade down the side of your face instead of running into your eyes. Start with a light smear at first; if this proves insufficient, slap on a little more. Vaseline do a handy size tin for your training bag at around £1. Also apply to any body parts to prevent chafing while training – I think you can guess which regions I am referring to.

Dave and Brandon Birkett training together

It's never too young to learn, and working on the pads helps strength and co-ordination for throwing and racquet sports as well as martial arts. It is an ideal way of finding out if the child has a liking for martial arts; a child should never be 'pushed' into doing it.

Here we see young Brandon Birkett training with his dad, Dave, who manages The Dartford Academy of Martial Arts, which runs a similar programme of martial arts training for boys and girls as does The Bob Breen Academy in London.

(Enquiries; The Bob Breen Academy, Hoxton, London 0207 729 5789; The Dartford Academy of Martial Arts, Dartford, Kent 01322 229124.)

In the scene depicted above, Dave is actually rejoicing in the fact he has dragged the little rascal away from the Playstation for ten minutes.

Thanks to our Models

Dave Birkett

Shereen Rowe

Brandon Birkett

Wayne Rowlands

Owen Ogbourne

Stephanie De Howes

Victoria Mose

Corey Donoghue

Workouts

Punchbags and focus pads – the workouts

These workouts involve exercises which most people who have spent time at a gym will be familiar with, but to clear up any mystery I have included photos for them.

Press-ups/ Push ups

Curl ups

Reverse curls

Crunches

Step ups

Squats

Lunges

Box jumps

Substituting more favourable or acceptable exercises, to make things easier or more difficult, can easily change the workout I have tabulated, it is your choice. I would, however, always advocate changing *any* workout after it starts to become easier; only exercise of a slightly challenging, or demanding nature will be likely to bring about a marked improvement. If your body gets accustomed to routines to the point where they are comfortable, you are unlikely to get much more than maintenance from your training. Providing you are reasonably healthy and not totally unfit it pays to stretch yourself a little.

I have made the assumption that more than one type of bag is available, for which you will be unlikely to thank me if all you have before you is a heavy bag of the 'collosus' variety, in which case you should finish up as a truly powerful hitter, so all may not be lost.

THE SOLO WORKOUT

Tables are provided on the following pages for you to complete, and also to photocopy when you run out.

Task	
1.	Skip
2.	Shadow box
3.	Short stretch (as per the 'stretching' section & joint mobilisation (hips, knees, ankles, wrists, neck and shoulders) i.e GET LOOSE!
4.	Light bag – hit fast and light, moving around bag as much as possible
5.	Skip – Fast tempo
6.	Abs – reverse curls
7.	Teardrop or double-ended bag, straight punches, hooks & uppercuts
8.	Press-ups
9.	Skip at maximum speed, 'running in place' technique
10.	Step-ups;
11.	Shadow box
12.	Heavy bag – hitting solidly
13.	Box jumps
14.	Skip
15.	Squats – 20 reps
16.	Floor-to-ceiling ball or speedball
17.	Shuttle run
18.	Crunches
19.	Press-ups
20.	Light bag – fast, firm hitting with combinations
21.	Lunges – 20 reps (in total)

Beginners	Done?	Intermediate	Done?	Advanced	Done?
2 mins		3 mins		3 mins	
2 mins		3 mins		3 mins	
2 mins		2 mins		2 mins	
1 min		2 mins		2 mins	
10		20		30	
2 mins		2 mins		2 mins	
15		25		30-40	
30 secs		1 min		2 mins	
20: empty hands		30: 5kg dumbbells		40: 5-10kg dumbbells	
2 mins		2 mins		2 mins	
2 mins		2 mins		2 mins	
30 secs		1 min		2 mins	
2 mins		2 mins		2 mins	
empty hands		5-10kg dumbbells		10-20kg dumbbells	
2 mins		2 mins		2 mins	
2 mins		2 mins		2 mins	
20		30		40-50	
15		25		30-40 with feet elevated	
2 mins		2 mins		2 mins	
empty hands		5-10kg dumbbells		10-20kg dumbbells	

Task	
1.	Skip
2.	Shadow box
3.	Short stretch (as per the 'stretching' section & joint mobilisation – hips, knees, ankles, wrists, neck and shoulders) i.e GET LOOSE!
4.	Light bag – hit fast and light, moving around bag as much as possible
5.	Skip – Fast tempo
6.	Abs – reverse curls
7.	Teardrop or double-ended bag, straight punches, hooks & uppercuts
8.	Press-ups
9.	Skip at maximum speed, 'running in place' technique
10.	Step-ups
11.	Shadow box
12.	Heavy bag – hitting solidly
13.	Box jumps
14.	Skip
15.	Squats – 20 reps
16.	Floor-to-ceiling ball or speedball
17.	Shuttle run
18.	Crunches
19.	Press-ups
20.	Light bag – fast, firm hitting with combinations
21.	Lunges – 20 reps (in total)

Beginners	Done?	Intermediate	Done?	Advanced	Done?
2 mins		3 mins		3 mins	
2 mins		3 mins		3 mins	
2 mins		2 mins		2 mins	
1 min		2 mins		2 mins	
10		20		30	
2 mins		2 mins		2 mins	
15		25		30-40	
30 secs		1 min		2 mins	
20: empty hands		30: 5kg dumbbells		40: 5-10kg dumbbells	
2 mins		2 mins		2 mins	
2 mins		2 mins		2 mins	
30 secs		1 min		2 mins	
2 mins		2 mins		2 mins	
empty hands		5-10kg dumbbells		10-20kg dumbbells	
2 mins		2 mins		2 mins	
2 mins		2 mins		2 mins	
20		30		40-50	
15		25		30-40 with feet elevated	
2 mins		2 mins		2 mins	
empty hands		5-10kg dumbbells		10-20kg dumbbells	

Date: ....

	Task
1.	Skip
2.	Shadow box
3.	Short stretch (as per the 'stretching' section & joint mobilisation (hips, knees, ankles, wrists, neck and shoulders) i.e GET LOOSE!
4.	Light bag – hit fast and light, moving around bag as much as possible
5.	Skip – Fast tempo
6.	Abs – reverse curls
7.	Teardrop or double-ended bag, straight punches, hooks & uppercuts
8.	Press-ups
9.	Skip at maximum speed, 'running in place' technique
10.	Step-ups;
11.	Shadow box
12.	Heavy bag – hitting solidly
13.	Box jumps
14.	Skip
15.	Squats – 20 reps
16.	Floor-to-ceiling ball or speedball
17.	Shuttle run
18.	Crunches
19.	Press-ups
20.	Light bag – fast, firm hitting with combinations
21.	Lunges – 20 reps (in total)

Beginners	Done?	Intermediate	Done?	Advanced	Done?
2 mins		3 mins		3 mins	
2 mins		3 mins		3 mins	
2 mins		2 mins		2 mins	
1 min		2 mins		2 mins	
10		20		30	
2 mins		2 mins		2 mins	
15		25		30-40	
30 secs		1 min		2 mins	
20: empty hands		30: 5kg dumbbells		40: 5-10kg dumbbells	
2 mins		2 mins		2 mins	
2 mins		2 mins		2 mins	
30 secs		1 min		2 mins	
2 mins		2 mins		2 mins	
empty hands		5-10kg dumbbells		10-20kg dumbbells	
2 mins		2 mins		2 mins	
2 mins		2 mins		2 mins	
20		30		40-50	
15		25		30-40 with feet elevated	
2 mins		2 mins		2 mins	
empty hands		5-10kg dumbbells		10-20kg dumbbells	

Date: ....

Task	
1.	Skip
2.	Shadow box
3.	Short stretch (as per the 'stretching' section & joint mobilisation (hips, knees, ankles, wrists, neck and shoulders) i.e GET LOOSE!
4.	Light bag – hit fast and light, moving around bag as much as possible
5.	Skip – Fast tempo
6.	Abs – reverse curls
7.	Teardrop or double-ended bag, straight punches, hooks & uppercuts
8.	Press-ups
9.	Skip at maximum speed, 'running in place' technique
10.	Step-ups;
11.	Shadow box
12.	Heavy bag – hitting solidly
13.	Box jumps
14.	Skip
15.	Squats – 20 reps
16.	Floor-to-ceiling ball or speedball
17.	Shuttle run
18.	Crunches
19.	Press-ups
20.	Light bag – fast, firm hitting with combinations
21.	Lunges – 20 reps (in total)

Beginners	Done?	Intermediate	Done?	Advanced	Done?
2 mins		3 mins		3 mins	
2 mins		3 mins		3 mins	
2 mins		2 mins		2 mins	
I min		2 mins		2 mins	
10		20		30	
2 mins		2 mins		2 mins	
15		25		30-40	
30 secs		I min		2 mins	
20: empty hands		30: 5kg dumbbells		40: 5-10kg dumbbells	
2 mins		2 mins		2 mins	
2 mins		2 mins		2 mins	
30 secs		I min		2 mins	
2 mins		2 mins		2 mins	
empty hands		5-10kg dumbbells		10-20kg dumbbells	
2 mins		2 mins		2 mins	
2 mins		2 mins		2 mins	
20		30		40-50	
15		25		30-40 with feet elevated	
2 mins		2 mins		2 mins	
empty hands		5-10kg dumbbells		10-20kg dumbbells	

Date: ....

	Task
1.	Skip
2.	Shadow box
3.	Short stretch (as per the 'stretching' section & joint mobilisation (hips, knees, ankles, wrists, neck and shoulders) i.e GET LOOSE!
4.	Light bag – hit fast and light, moving around bag as much as possible
5.	Skip – Fast tempo
6.	Abs – reverse curls
7.	Teardrop or double-ended bag, straight punches, hooks & uppercuts
8.	Press-ups
9.	Skip at maximum speed, 'running in place' technique
10.	Step-ups;
11.	Shadow box
12.	Heavy bag – hitting solidly
13.	Box jumps
14.	Skip
15.	Squats – 20 reps
16.	Floor-to-ceiling ball or speedball
17.	Shuttle run
18.	Crunches
19.	Press-ups
20.	Light bag – fast, firm hitting with combinations
21.	Lunges – 20 reps (in total)

Beginners	Done?	Intermediate	Done?	Advanced	Done?
2 mins		3 mins		3 mins	
2 mins		3 mins		3 mins	
2 mins		2 mins		2 mins	
1 min		2 mins		2 mins	
10		20		30	
2 mins		2 mins		2 mins	
15		25		30-40	
30 secs		1 min		2 mins	
20: empty hands		30: 5kg dumbbells		40: 5-10kg dumbbells	
2 mins		2 mins		2 mins	
2 mins		2 mins		2 mins	
30 secs		1 min		2 mins	
2 mins		2 mins		2 mins	
empty hands		5-10kg dumbbells		10-20kg dumbbells	
2 mins		2 mins		2 mins	
2 mins		2 mins		2 mins	
20		30		40-50	
15		25		30-40 with feet elevated	
2 mins		2 mins		2 mins	
empty hands		5-10kg dumbbells		10-20kg dumbbells	

Training notes